Places of
Musical Fame

Places of
Musical Fame

By SHARON LERNER

Illustrated by GEORGE OVERLIE

Prepared under the supervision of Robert W. Surplus

Musical Books for Young People

LERNER PUBLICATIONS COMPANY
MINNEAPOLIS, MINNESOTA

Revised Edition 1967

International Copyright Secured. Printed in U.S.A.

Library of Congress Catalog Card Number: 62-20803

Second Printing 1963
Third Printing 1964
Fourth Printing 1965
Fifth Printing 1967
Sixth Printing 1968

Contents

MORE THAN
FOUR WALLS AND A CEILING

A great deal has been written about music and composers, but little has been written about the places in which music is performed. This book tells about some of the great concert halls and opera houses of the world.

No claim is made that these are all the most important places in which music is performed, although some of the most famous are included. Instead, these are concert halls and opera houses which we have found interesting and which we have chosen to share with you.

A concert hall or an opera house is more than just four walls and a ceiling. The lives, hopes, and careers of many people are closely tied up with any place of musical fame. Famous musicians, conductors, and stagehands all add to tradition that is a part of each hall.

But by far the most important thing about a concert hall is: *How good does music sound in it?* Architects know that how they plan a hall determines how good the sound will be. They give careful attention to a number of important details.

5

What are some of the things that receive careful attention? Here is a list of some of them.

Seats—Plush or soft seats are used since they absorb, or take in sound.

Size—The hall cannot be too large or the sound will be lost. A hall with 1,500 to 2,200 seats is considered a good size. Also, a hall shaped like a rectangle seems to have the best sound.

Ceiling—A flat ceiling with some kind of panels to absorb sound is usually used.

Absorbent Materials—Materials that absorb sound are often used to stop slow echoes. Draperies and plaster with a lot of air bubbles are two such materials.

Interruptions in Sound Path—Anything in the path of the sound is avoided. Posts and columns are not found in the newest halls. Plans are made so everyone can see as well as hear all that goes on.

Outside Noises—A good hall is planned so that outside noises do not disturb the listener.

Furnishings—Everything put into a hall is chosen not only for how it looks but also for how it will affect sound. Care is taken that nothing in the hall will start to vibrate with the music.

Good Low Register—A hall that makes low notes sound rich and full is best.

High Reverberation Time—The best concert halls have a reverberation, or echo time, of 1.8 to 2.0 seconds.

Balcony—The balcony should not extend over the seats on the first floor. Sound will not reach these seats properly if it does.

Balance and Blending—The music should not only sound well to the audience, but it should also sound balanced and blended to the musicians on stage.

As you read about some of the famous concert halls and opera houses, think about how many things had to be considered in building them. Remember that many people's minds, talents, and lives went into the planning and building of these places. A concert hall is more than four walls and a ceiling!

LINCOLN CENTER

One of New York's older neighborhoods is suddenly changing as Lincoln Center goes up. New Yorkers are proud of the new Lincoln Center for the Performing Arts. This huge project will cost over 165 million dollars and will be the home of the finest in the world of music, drama, and dance.

Five buildings make up Lincoln Center. They are Philharmonic Hall, Metropolitan Opera House, New York State Theater, Vivian Beaumont Theater, and the Juilliard Building.

7

Philharmonic Hall

Max Abramovitz, the man who designed this $15,400,000 building was told by the board of directors, "This hall is expected to be the finest musical instrument in the world." A concert hall is as important to good music as are the instruments of the orchestra playing there.

We all know that *listening* is most important in a concert hall, since you are there mainly to *hear* a concert. In order to make Philharmonic Hall perfect for listening, experts in *acoustics*, or the science of sound,were asked to find out what makes a concert hall good for listening. The experts studied the acoustics of 30 of the best-liked concert halls in the world and talked to many leading conductors. They tried to find out why conditions for sound in some halls were better than others. They asked about size, shape, stages, number of seats and balconies, ceilings, floors, and *reverberations* (the rebounds,or the bouncing of sounds off the walls). Taking all these different ideas and learning from the mistakes of other designers, the architects set out to plan Philharmonic Hall, the most perfect listening hall in the world.

Philharmonic Hall is the permanent home of America's oldest orchestra, the New York Philharmonic. This fine hall, whose 70-foot windows run from street to roof, was opened in 1962. It was the first concert hall built in New York city since Carnegie Hall was built in 1891.

As you probably guessed, the acoustics in this modern hall are very unusual. Hanging from the ceiling of the auditorium are 136 especially designed sound panels arranged to give even sound everywhere. The hall must be "tuned" before each concert by adjusting these sound panels. For everyone in the 2,646 seats, hearing is excellent, and all have a clear view of the stage.

The stage is 61 feet wide by 40 feet *deep,* the distance from the front of the stage to the back, and easily holds the full 106-piece Philharmonic Orchestra. There is a 98-rank pipe organ behind and along side the stage. The hall is air conditioned and is used all year around.

Philharmonic Hall was designed for many purposes. The stage can be lowered for "pop" concerts, or concerts where light music is played. A large movie screen can be used for films. A smaller television screen can be placed above the orchestra during children's concerts, so the audience can have a close-up view of the players.

9

Metropolitan Opera House

The Metropolitan Opera House is easy to pick out as it has five arches in its front. It is the new home of the Metropolitan Opera Company, which has played for many years in the historic old "Met."

The opera house was designed by Wallace K. Harrison and cost $45,700,000 to build. It is air-conditioned for year-round performances and seats 3,800 people. There are four stages; a main stage, with three other stages—one on each side and one in the back, so that several operas can be set up at once.

10

New York State Theater

New York State Theater is a center for dance and operetta. During the New York World's Fair in 1964-65 this building was used for the State of New York exhibits.

The building was designed by Philip Johnson. The auditorium has three *balconies,* or upper rings of seats, and holds 2,800 people. All the seats have a fine view of the stage, and hearing conditions are excellent.

Vivian Beaumont Theater

The Vivian Beaumont Theater, named for the woman who gave a large amount of money for its building, is the home of the Lincoln Repertory Company. A *repertory company* is one group of actors and actresses who work together to put on many different kinds of plays.

The theater was designed by Eero Saarinen. It is built so that the size and shape of the stage can be changed for different kinds of plays. At no time is anyone in the audience more than 65 feet away from the stage. Everyone can have a good seat at the Vivian Beaumont Theater.

Lincoln Center Library-Museum

This combination library and museum is in the Beaumont Theater. It contains 500,000 phonograph records, more than 500,000 books and magazines, and thousands of other interesting materials. The children's room is especially designed for puppet shows as well as reading.

12

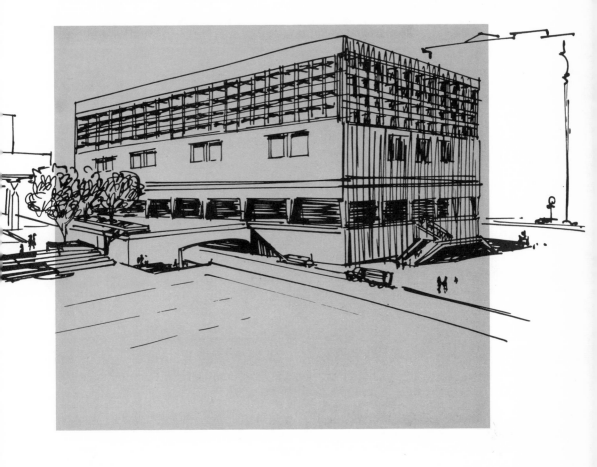

Juilliard Building

The Juilliard Building will house one of America's best known music schools—the Juilliard School of Music. Courses in music, drama, and dance will be taught here. There will be many practice and rehearsal halls as well as rooms for 200 students to live in while studying at the school. An attractive restaurant for both indoor and outdoor eating will be a part of the building.

CARNEGIE HALL

Carnegie Hall is more than a building! It is a world music center and has been the place of personal success for hundreds of famous people. Around the concert hall are the apartments and studios of artists, musicians, dancers, and writers. Carnegie Hall was the home of the New York Philharmonic Orchestra until it moved to Lincoln Center.

Carnegie Hall was built in 1891 by Andrew Carnegie, a millionaire steel manufacturer who gave two million dollars for its construction. The large, stone auditorium was designed by William Burnet Tuthill. At first, the auditorium, with its two levels of *box seats,* or choice groups of seats, and two balconies, seated 3,000 people and had standing room for several hundred more. Now, New York City fire laws have limited the spectators to 2,760, plus room for a small standing audience. At the time of the building's construction, the sound was not considered to be very good, but later it was improved.

The Music Hall, as it was called for its first few years, opened on May 5, 1891, with a five day music festival. Peter Tchaikovsky, the famous composer, came from Russia for the occasion to conduct some of his own works. Many other important music personalities have made history at Carnegie Hall. It was here that Jascha Heifetz, the world-renowned violinist, made his debut before a sell-out crowd in 1917, when he was 16 years old. Van Cliburn, the American pianist who first became famous in Russia, played at Carnegie Hall in May, 1958 to an audience in which there were people willing to pay 150 dollars for a ticket. Here, in this important music hall, Arturo Toscanini, at the age of 87, conducted his last concert after 68 years of directing. Fritz Kreisler, the brilliant violinist who died in 1961 said, "I feel that Carnegie Hall is my real home in New York."

Carnegie Hall was to be torn down after the completion of Lincoln Center, but so many people protested that New York's Governor, Nelson Rockefeller, signed a law which saved the building.

METROPOLITAN OPERA HOUSE

The famous Metropolitan Opera House is no longer the home of the Metropolitan Opera Company. The "Met" has moved to Lincoln Center. This old building, however, has a colorful past and a very important name in music. Many of the world's greatest singers have sung in its halls. To sing at the "Met" has been the goal of many young opera performers.

A New York landmark, the "Met" first opened its doors on October 22, 1883. It was designed by Josiah Cleaveland Cady on an entire city block. Built of dull yellow brick, the "Met" was not very attractive on the outside, but the beautiful interior could be compared to the famous opera houses of Europe. Rows of comfortable dark red velvet chairs lined the main floor and the five balconies. The lower balconies formed the famous "Diamond Horseshoe," the best seats in the house. The "Met" seated 3,616 people. The acoustics were very good, with no microphones needed to carry the music to the far corners of the house. A great golden curtain covered the large stage which could hold over 100 people during one opera. The stage measured 72 feet wide and 100 feet high.

16

During one opera season, over 540,000 people attended shows at the "Met." Students from all over the New York area attended special performances which were very popular. At these concerts, the "Met" presented an opera that was easily understood. It was very exciting to attend such a performance and watch the eager faces.

Each year, the traveling Metropolitan Opera Company goes to people who can't come to New York. It takes over 300 people in two special trains and goes on a yearly spring tour, giving concerts throughout the United States.

Of all the operas presented at the "Met", the five which have been performed most are *Aida*, with over 400 performances, *La Boheme*, *Carmen*, *Faust* and *Lohengrin*, each with more than 300 showings.

Opera in America owes much to the famous old "Met".

ACADEMY OF MUSIC

The Academy of Music is the home of the Philadelphia Symphony Orchestra. This well-loved concert hall was built in 1856.

The architects, Napoleon Le Brun and Gustavus Runge, planned the outside of the Academy to look like the famous La Scala Opera of Milan, Italy. Le Brun thought that the heart of a concert hall is in its fine sound. The acoustics at the Academy are so good that when every seat is filled you can hear a pin drop on the stage.

Le Brun did many strange things to make the Academy's sound so perfect. Two large domes were built, one forming the ceiling and one under the floor. The walls in the front and back were rounded. This was done to keep the sound from getting lost in a corner. Cows' hair was put into the plaster walls to help keep the sound in the auditorium. Only the four main walls of the building were put up at first, and for one year, the rain, snow, and sun beat down on them so they would dry, or "season", perfectly. Then the roof was put up.

The lobby is very attractive, with tall white and gold columns and many pots of ferns. A long stairway leads to the auditorium which holds 3,200 people. There are three balconies arranged in a horseshoe shape. A large chandelier with long strings of shiny crystal beads hangs from the ceiling.

There have been many concerts by great orchestras and opera companies at the Academy. Such well known artists as Caruso, Melba, and Toscanini have performed here.

During its history, lots of events have taken place at the Academy that were not musical. In 1872, U. S. Grant was renominated there for a second term for president of the United States. A football game was once played there and, at one time, prize cattle were shown.

There are many stories about the Academy of Music. One story tells of a bat which flies around the building every time music by Beethoven is played. Do you believe it?

CONSTITUTION HALL

Constitution Hall is located across the park from the White House. It is considered the cultural center of our nation's capital, although there is now talk of a new and much larger center. This handsome building was designed by John Russell Pope in 1938. It is owned and operated by the *National Society of the Daughters of the American Revolution,* an organization of women who work for patriotic causes.

The building is constructed of Alabama limestone and has a beautiful entrance. There is a broad stairway and eight high columns or pillars in the lobby. The U-shaped auditorium has balconies on two sides and one at the end. The side balconies slope down to the main floor. Buff and blue, the colors of the D.A.R., are used throughout the building. About 4,000 people can be comfortably seated in the concert hall. The acoustics are practically perfect.

Constitution Hall is the home of the National Symphony Orchestra and is used by the orchestra for practice. They present about 70 concerts a year in the hall. Many other symphony orchestras from the United States and Canada have played there, and many famous performers have performed there. The building is also often used as a lecture hall.

It must be thrilling to attend a concert at Constitution Hall on the same night that the President of the United States is there.

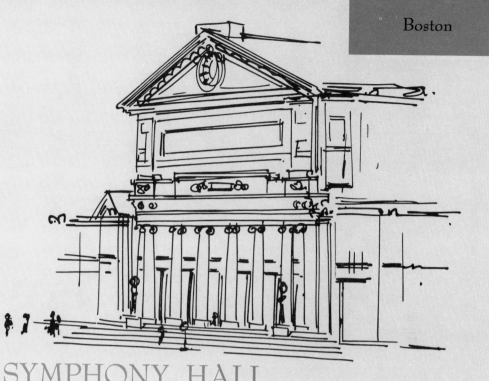

SYMPHONY HALL

Symphony Hall, constructed just before the turn of the century, is the home of the Boston Symphony Orchestra.

The building, designed by McKim, Meade, and White of New York City, was planned to be very similar to the famous old Boston Music Hall. The acoustics of the Music Hall were copied in Symphony Hall. The building is attractively decorated and has many up-to-date improvements. Symphony Hall seats 2,631 people in the winter and 2,345 in May and June when there are "pop" concerts.

The famous Boston Symphony Orchestra gives about 60 concerts a season here. In addition to this, Symphony Hall is used for other orchestras, choruses, solo recitals, jazz concerts, radio and television broadcasts, public and private meetings, religious services, conventions, political rallies, high school and college commencements, fashion shows, banquets, and trade shows.

21

SAN FRANCISCO OPERA HOUSE

The San Francisco Opera House is the home of the famous and important San Francisco Opera Company and the San Francisco Symphony Orchestra. Opened in 1932, this opera house, sometimes called the War Memorial Opera House, is one of the newest concert halls in the United States.

Ever since the days of the Gold Rush, good music has been very popular in San Francisco. During the years 1850-1860, one historian said that there was more music and murder in San Francisco than in any other city in the world. At that time, there wasn't a suitable concert hall where music could be heard. Many times money was raised to build a grand concert hall. The famous 1906 earthquake ended one attempt. Finally, in 1926, the San Francisco Opera House was started.

22

The opera house is located in the Civic Center of San Francisco. This beautiful structure is built of greyish white stone, and all the floors are shiny marble. Two broad stairways lead up to the gold and white auditorium. The large chandelier that hangs from the ceiling looks like a lighted star. It is a big auditorium, with seats for 3,252 people. The stage is 83 feet deep and 131 feet wide.

Some world-famous events have taken place at the San Francisco Opera. Here, in 1945, the United Nations was born. The Japanese Peace Treaty of 1951 was signed in this building. Many, many great singers such as Lily Pons, Ezio Pinza, and Lauritz Melchior have performed here, to name just a few.

23

THE PALACE OF FINE ARTS

The Palace of Fine Arts is the most important concert hall and art gallery in Mexico. The auditorium is used for opera, symphony, folk dancing, ballet, and presidential inaugurations. The art gallery houses great paintings and sculpture by many important artists. Among them are the famous murals of Mexico's Diego Rivera.

This building, constructed of white marble, was started in 1900 but was not completed until 1934. The building was set on soft ground and has sunk about 15 feet. There is now a noticeable slant to the building.

The interior is panelled with handsome native wood. A Tiffany glass curtain designed by a Mexican artist covers the spacious stage. This magnificent curtain shows two volcanos. The curtain is not used too often because it can only be moved by machinery. The theater seats about 2,000 people.

24

COLÓN THEATER

The *Colón* Theater is the center of Buenos Aires' cultural life and the most important opera house in South America. It was named after Christopher Columbus, the discoverer of America. In Spanish, his name was *Cristóbal Colón*. This government-owned and operated concert hall was opened in 1908.

During the music season, which runs from May until October, many internationally known musicians perform. Opera, ballet, and symphony concerts are presented by the theater's own company. Many foreign casts bring the best in opera to the Colón Theater.

The stately building has a large lobby with beautiful big windows. A long stairway leads to the auditorium which seats about 3,500 people. The concert hall has a very noble and dignified feeling about it.

25

COVENT GARDEN

In 1732, John Rich built the first Covent Garden on a piece of land that had once been a Catholic convent garden. Although Covent is not spelled exactly like convent, this is how the concert hall got its unusual name. The first Covent Garden was a very small theater. It was here, in 1766, that the first strike in theater history took place, because the ballet dancers refused to wear wool stockings instead of the usual silk.

On September 19, 1808, a stove pipe overheated, and within minutes the first Covent Garden was burned down. Almost one year after the first theater was destroyed, the second Covent Garden was opened on September 18, 1809. This new Covent Garden was the largest theater in Europe, until it, too, burned to the ground in 1856 after a crowd attending a masked ball had left.

The third, or present Covent Garden, was opened in 1858. It seats 2,000 people and is known for its good acoustics. The stage is 90 feet deep and 50 feet high. It is the home of the Royal Ballet Company and Covent Garden Opera Company.

The appearance of the building has changed little since it was built over 100 years ago. Red and gold are still the colors of the horseshoe-shaped concert hall, and Queen Victoria's picture still looks down upon the audience. The Royal Opera House, as it has sometimes been called, has a cozy feeling that makes people enjoy themselves. In the lobby is a red carpet to dry your feet during the rainy season.

At opening night performances, or at special events, the Royal Box is used by England's Royal Family. A private dining room is attached to the box, and there is a separate entrance from the street. At coronation times and during the Edwardian period, programs were printed on silk.

During both World Wars Covent Garden was closed as a theater. In World War I, it was used as a furniture warehouse and in World War II, as a dance hall.

Visitors to London are surprised to see Covent Garden located among the fruit, flower, and vegetable stands in one of the world's largest markets. Opera fans have to pick their way through the stalls of tomatoes, gladioli, and pineapples to get to Covent Garden.

PARIS OPERA

Paris Opera, sometimes called *Palais Garnier,* was designed by Charles Garnier. Construction was started in 1861 by order of Napoleon III. When the outside walls and roof were completed in 1870, the work had to be stopped because of the Franco-Prussian War. The unfinished building was used for food storage, and the roof was used for launching balloons. The balloons were Paris' only means of outside communication, since the Prussian army had surrounded the city.

After the war, it was discovered that the Paris Opera was actually built over a huge underground lake. Construction had to be delayed one more year so the lake could be drained. The Paris Opera was finally completed in 1874, and from that time on has been the most important cultural center in Paris.

Today, the interior of the Paris Opera is as beautiful as when it was first built. Inside the main entrance there is a large and very impressive stairway of white marble. The railings of the stairway are made of carved stone from Algeria. On top of these railings are marble statues which hold up chandeliers. The walls are made of marble, and most of the floors are *mosaic,* or glass tiles. There are statues of famous French composers, writers, and artists along the corridors. The ceilings are covered with *frescos*, or pictures painted in wet plaster.

The main red and gold concert hall is round. It is lighted by a huge center chandelier that contains 1,600 light bulbs. Ten small chandeliers help light this great hall. The Paris Opera has the largest stage in the world, measuring 125 feet deep, 100 feet long, and 200 feet high. Because of the large size of the stage, many spectacular productions have been given. One long-remembered ballet performance had a spouting volcano that threw sponge rocks into the air, and a full-rigged ship that sailed on stage and then sank under canvas waves. With all its beauty, charm, and magnificent stage, the seating capacity of Paris Opera is surprisingly small, a disappointing 2,156.

The Paris Opera is owned and run by the French government. By government rule, two thirds of the operas performed must be composed by Frenchmen. Because of this, wonderful operas by Mozart, Wagner, and Verdi are rarely presented. Ninety per cent of the singers in any opera must be French, and choruses are paid extra if they sing in another language when a French version is available. Sometimes the chorus sings in French and the soloists in Italian. This can really confuse the listener!

Composers who have worked at this huge building at the head of the *Avenue de l'Opera* have made many comments about it. Claude DeBussy, the famous French composer, referred to the Paris Opera as a "Turkish bath". Dancer Serge Lifar said it looks like a "glorious cemetery", probably because of all the statues that are found throughout the building.

OPÉRA-COMIQUE

Paris' *Opéra-Comique* stands out among opera houses. It is a small theater, seating only about 1,500 people. This smallness is very nice for audiences. They can be closer to the stage and feel more a part of the opera. Because of this, many operas which would be lost in a large opera house are successfully performed here.

The Opéra-Comique has a history dating back to 1714. The group played in many theaters, but it wasn't until May, 1840, that they moved to the present site on the *Boulevard des Italians*. The concert hall was made by reconstructing an old theater that had fallen into ruin. Beautifully rebuilt, the opera house was a very popular and an important place for opera productions.

31

Many great opera *premieres*, or openings, took place at the Opéra-Comique. Probably the most important occurred on March 3, 1875. This was the premier of Georges Bizet's famous opera, *Carmen*. The audience did not like *Carmen* too well, and by the fourth act it was sung to a nearly empty theater. With its second performance, *Carmen* began to gain peoples' interest, until today it has been performed over 3,000 times at the Opéra-Comique.

On the night of April 10, 1900, an event took place at the Opéra-Comique which marked the start of the career of a great opera singer, Mary Garden. Miss Garden was a stand-in for the leading lady in the opera, *Louise*. The *prima donna,* or leading lady, got sick, and Mary Garden took over her very difficult part. For this, Miss Garden received a standing ovation and went on to become a very famous singer.

The Opéra-Comique was destroyed by a fire in 1887. The present building was put up eleven years later, in 1898. This building looks like a smaller edition of its bigger neighbor, the Paris Opera. The Opéra-Comique has a large lobby with beautiful pictures and statues.

During intermission at the Opéra-Comique, slides are shown advertising places to visit for eating and shopping. The local people don't like this very much, but the tourists do.

LA SCALA

The *La Scala* Opera House was designed in 1776 by Giuseppe Piermarini, a well known architect who had just finished redesigning the Palace of Milan. The building was constructed on the spot that the ruined church of *Santa Maria alla Scala*, built in 1381, had stood. La Scala, named for the church, was opened on August 3, 1778. At that time it was believed to be the largest and most completely equipped theater of any kind in the world. In those days, opera was done in a big way. The opening night performance had 36 live horses on stage.

The opera house is constructed of brick and has a simple outside. Today, it looks very much as it did in 1778. The main concert hall is painted bright red, white, and gold. It is circular in shape and has six balconies that are divided into *boxes*. A huge center chandelier with 365 lights shines down from the ceiling. Over the stage is a very large clock whose hands are fun to watch since they move just every five minutes. La Scala has seats for 3,200 people.

At one time almost all of the boxes, or separate seating areas, were privately owned and were decorated to please the owners. Each box looked different—some had glass mirrors, painted frescos, and carved or gold ceilings. The walls were lined with tapestries and paintings showing scenes from the owner's favorite opera.

In the lobby there is a row of coffee shops, souvenir stands, and gambling tables. This is the only place where gambling is allowed in Milan, and only because money is raised for the theater here. In the same building there is a La Scala Museum, which has interesting objects connected with the history of music and drama.

During World War II La Scala was badly bombed, and only the outer walls were left standing. All the scenery and costumes for over 100 operas were destroyed. La Scala was rebuilt 3 years later and was reopened to look almost exactly as it had been.

From the time it was built, La Scala was mainly an opera house, although jugglers, acrobats, puppets, and tight rope walkers have performed here.

An audience at La Scala does not applaud at the end of an act or scene, but during the entire show they will boo or cheer according to how they feel about a performance. It must be very difficult to perform at La Scala for audiences will only listen to the very best.

La Scala has been the most important opera hall in the world, where success or failure had the most meaning to a performer or composer. Here the world premiere of Puccini's opera, *Madame Butterfly,* was held in 1904. The first night it played, it was booed so badly that Puccini went home and completely changed his opera. It had its second opening at La Scala and has since become one of the world's most popular and best loved operas.

SAN CARLO

The *San Carlo* opera house of Naples is the most stunning of all opera houses. The oldest of Italy's many opera halls, it was built in 1737 by order of Charles III of Bourbon, the ruler of Naples. The people of Naples were great opera fans, and this beautiful building made them very proud.

There was a strange and very strict rule at that time. No one in the audience was allowed to applaud at the end of an act or at the end of the entire show, and no *encores,* or extra numbers, could be presented. Only the king could applaud, and when he did the rest of the audience could join in.

San Carlo was redecorated several times during its history; once in 1768 because of the king's wedding, and a second time in 1816 when a lighted lantern started a fire that ruined the building. Within 6 days the rebuilding was started, and it was reopened one year later. The cost of the rebuilding was double the amount of the original hall. Today, San Carlo looks much the same as it did in 1817.

Visitors to Naples find the outside of San Carlo disappointing, as it is not much different from other large buildings in the city. But once inside, they see that it is an elegant place. The eye-catching lobby has highly polished marble pillars and floors, and everything is very clean and shiny. The concert hall is painted gold and white, and is decorated with statues, carvings, and frescos. There are five balconies which are divided into roomy and comfortable boxes. Between each box are four long electric candles covered by glass globes to provide the lighting. Before the use of electricity all the flaming candles were lovely to look at, but can you imagine the fire danger? Above the stage is a round clock which moves around a figure of Father Time. He looks as if he were trying to hold back "time". In the center of the hall is the Royal Box, which is connected to a corridor leading to the palace. This box has not been used for a long time, as Italy has no king now.

Many famous people have played and composed for San Carlo. When the famous composer, Mozart, wrote to his sister, at the age of 14, from San Carlo, he said, "The theater is beautiful!"

BAYREUTH FESTSPIELHAUS

Richard Wagner, the famous German composer, had a dream. He wanted to build an ideal concert hall in the country, at which music festivals could be held. This dream became known as *Bayreuth Festspielhaus*.

Wagner had a hard time getting support and money for his plan. He traveled throughout Europe conducting benefit concerts and selling his music. Other musicians such as the famous pianist, Franz Liszt, helped by giving performances. Wagner clubs were even started to raise money. Finally Ludwig, the mad king of Bavaria, gave Wagner the help he needed. Ludwig was fond of building palaces, and the idea of an opera house appealed to him.

On a rainy May 22, 1872, Wagner's fifty-ninth birthday, the cornerstone for the Festspielhaus was laid. That evening Wagner conducted Beethoven's *Ninth Symphony*, in the old Bayreuth opera house. Wagner wanted this proud masterpiece to be the symbol of his opera house. On August 2, 1873 the *Hebefeier* was held. This is the ceremony performed when the highest point of the building is reached before putting up the roof. Wagner climbed to the top while his *Tannhäuser March* was played below.

The Bayreuth Festspielhaus stands among beautiful wooded foothills. The town of Bayreuth and its castle and gardens are clearly seen. The town is just a fifteen minute walk away. Out

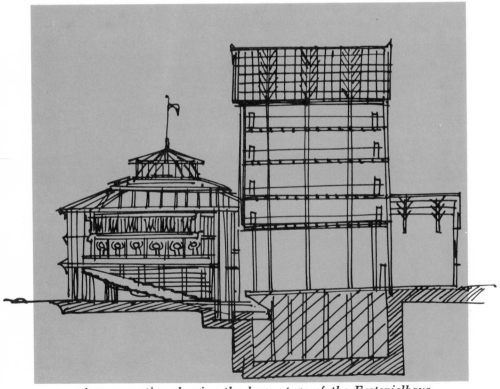

A cross section showing the huge stage of the Festspielhaus.

of view, but nearby, is Wagner's famous home — *Wahnfried.*
Today, buses and taxis take concert-goers up the hills to the
Festspielhaus, but in Wagner's day only two or three carriages
were for hire. Many richly dressed ladies walked the steep road
up to the theater.

The building is unusual looking, because Wagner planned
that it would only be temporary. The simple outside is brick,
and the interior is made of wood. Wagner had wanted an or-
nate stone structure, but that was too expensive.

For good listening, Wagner wanted to separate the musicians
and singers from the audience. To do this he put a huge
orchestra pit, or place where the musicians play, between the
stage and the audience. In this sunken orchestra pit, 165
invisible musicians could play.

The beams that line the auditorium are hollow wood, and
the ceiling is canvas. All this makes the acoustics excellent. The
stage is huge, and during a performance the theater is dark so
that all attention is on the stage. The concert hall is much the
same now as it was when it was completed, except that electricity
is now used for lighting. There are seats for over 1,800 people.

The Bayreuth Festspielhaus has had its ups and downs.
Money has always been a problem. At one time it was closed
for six years. During better times, great musicians such as Grieg,
Tchaikovsky, and Liszt, had come to hear Wagner's music. But
always the theater has been important in German music, and
thousands have enjoyed stirring concerts there. Wagner died in
1883, and was buried at Wahnfried. His wife, Cosima, carried on
the Festival, and with her son, Siegfried, brought fame to Bayreuth. During World Wars I and II the hall was not damaged,
and concerts for soldiers, and refugees were held there.

Today the temporary building that Wagner built has become
the permanent Bayreuth Festspielhaus.

STAATSOPER

Vienna is an unusual city. In no other place in the world has music been so important and have so many great composers and musicians lived and worked. Such outstanding men as Haydn, Mozart, Beethoven, Schubert, Wagner, Richard and Johann Strauss have all made Vienna their home. In this music-minded city most opera performances are given at the *Staatsoper,* or the State Opera.

The building of the Staatsoper began in 1860. This was a very bad time to build an opera house, because Austria was fighting a losing war with Italy. At the end of the war the government was in no mood to build an opera house. Finally, in 1869 the Staatsoper was completed and it opened on May 25. After its difficult start, the Staatsoper enjoyed years of musical success under the leadership of men like Johann Strauss, Gustav Mahler, and Bruno Walter.

On March 13, 1945, just three weeks before the end of World War II, the Staatsoper was bombed. The stage and the main auditorium were completely destroyed. After three days of flames, only the lobby and the main stairway were left standing. All the scenery and props for 120 operas, over 160,000 costumes, and many valuable musical instruments were lost. The people of Vienna were very sad about this great loss and went to work quickly to rebuild the Staatsoper. During the rebuilding, 150 carloads of scrap iron and 5,000 tons of rubble were taken away.

Finally, on November 5, 1955, the new Staatsoper was opened. The new opera house was rebuilt to look very much like the old one. Red, white, and gold are the colors of the concert hall. A huge crystal chandelier hangs from the center of the ceiling.

During the opera season, which lasts from September to June, an opera is performed every night. Tickets are reasonably priced and almost always sold out. Opera in Vienna is very popular with young people. They buy the lowest priced seats for the fourth balcony and during the show they boo or cheer for their favorite *arias,* or songs. Opera is Austria's main tourist attraction. It is said that, "In Vienna going to the opera is as common as going to church."

BOLSHOI THEATER

The *Bolshoi* Theater, or "great theater" is the most important theater in Russia. This impressive Greek styled building stands on *Sverdlow Square*, one of the central squares of Moscow. The Bolshoi Theater is the home of one of the world's greatest ballet companies, the Bolshoi Ballet. The Bolshoi Ballet is the leading cultural attraction in Russia.

44

The Bolshoi Ballet was started in 1776 in a private home. In 1805 it was moved to a larger theater building, but this burned down soon after the group settled there. The Bolshoi Ballet moved to the present Bolshoi Theater when it was built in 1856. It is a very big building, well known for its huge stage. The stage is very deep, wide and smooth, perfect for the dancers of the Bolshoi Ballet. Opera and symphony are also presented on this stage.

The beautiful auditorium is painted red, white and gold. In the middle of the concert hall is the Czar's, or king's box. From this box, the finest view of the stage is possible. The walls of the box are covered with red silk, just as it was in the days of the Czar. Nowadays, visiting diplomats and guests of the government sit here.

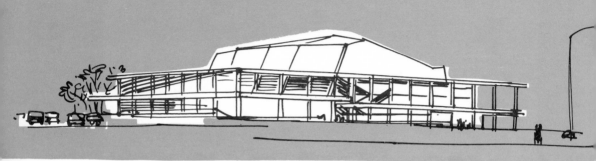

FREDRIC R. MANN AUDITORIUM

The Mann Auditorium is the finest and most important music center in the Middle East. The "Temple of Culture", as it is sometimes called, is the home of the famous Israel Philharmonic Orchestra. The building was named for Fredric R. Mann, a generous man from Philadelphia who gave a large amount of money for its construction.

The auditorium is part of a cultural center which includes an art gallery, and the *Habimah* Theater, the home of an outstanding group of theatrical players. The outside of the Mann Auditorium is very simple and impressive. Inside, the concert hall is fan-shaped and can seat 2,920 people. The fan-shaped auditorium provides for excellent acoustics, and there is always a good view of the stage from every seat. The balcony is a part of the sloping main floor.

The colors of the auditorium are very restful. Ash wood panelling covers the walls, the arched ceiling is grey, and the seats, imported from the United States, are black. The stage can hold as many as 120 musicians at one time.

The beautiful lobby surrounding the concert hall has glass walls and tall marble columns. Art shows, receptions, and dances are held in this lobby.

Of all the foreign concert halls mentioned in this book, the Mann Auditorium is the youngest. It was opened on October 1, 1957. At the opening, Leonard Bernstein conducted the Israel Philharmonic, and pianist Artur Rubinstein, violinist Isaac Stern, and cellist Paul Tortelier played. Many "greats" in the music world, such as conductor Dimitri Mitropoulos and violinists Yehudi Menuhin and Nathan Milstein, have played here. The auditorium is also used for opera, ballet, art festivals, folk dancing, and public meetings.

The Mann Auditorium is a bright spot for music in the Middle East. Nowhere else, for hundreds of miles, can music be heard in such an outstanding auditorium.

KABUKIZA

The *Kabukiza* in Tokyo is considered the best theater in Japan for the performance of *Kabuki*. The Kabukiza Theater was modernized in 1950 and is known as the home of Kabuki. Here, leading Kabuki actors perform. The exterior of the building is Japanese in style, but the inside is modern. It seats 2,600 people, and the lighting is very good.

The Kabukiza is not like a theater as we think of it. It has a revolving stage that goes around like a merry-go-round. This makes changing scenes very simple, as the stage just circles to the next set. No curtains are used to mark the end of an act. Much of Kabuki is played on a *hanamichi*. A hanamichi is a runway from the stage that goes through the audience.

Kabuki started in the sixteenth century. It is one of the most popular and important forms of entertainment in Japan. The players in Kabuki are always men. They even take the parts of women. Kabuki is presented in a very old style. All speech is very rhythmical and accompanied by music that is played off-stage. Costumes and scenery are brightly and beautifully colored.

Kabuki is an echo of Japan's past, and at the Kabukiza Theater it is presented true to the old ways.

48

ABOUT THE AUTHOR

Sharon Lerner has been able to combine her major interests of travel, music, and art in *Places of Musical Fame*. She has traveled throughout the United States, Mexico, Europe and the Middle East and has actually visited many of these famous places. Born and reared in Chicago, she later moved to Minneapolis where she graduated in Art Education from the University of Minnesota. She has taught at the Minneapolis Art Institute, Walker Art Center, University High School, and in the White Bear public school system. Mrs. Lerner is the author and illustrator of several other books: *The Self-Portrait in Art, I Found a Leaf, I Like Vegetables, I Picked a Flower,* and *Who Will Wake Up Spring?* She lives with her husband and son in Minneapolis.

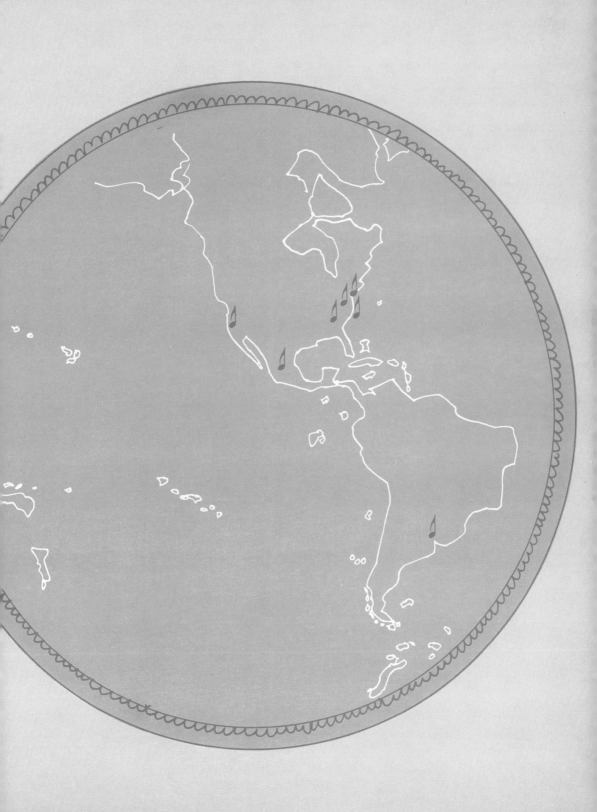

We specialize in publishing quality books for
young people. For a complete list please write

LERNER PUBLICATIONS COMPANY

241 First Avenue North, Minneapolis, Minnesota 55401